United States
Department of
Agriculture

Forest Service

Southern
Research Station

General Technical
Report SRS–122

Numerical Details and SAS Programs for Parameter Recovery of the S$_B$ Distribution

I0435598

Bernard R. Parresol, Teresa Fidalgo Fonseca,
and Carlos Pacheco Marques

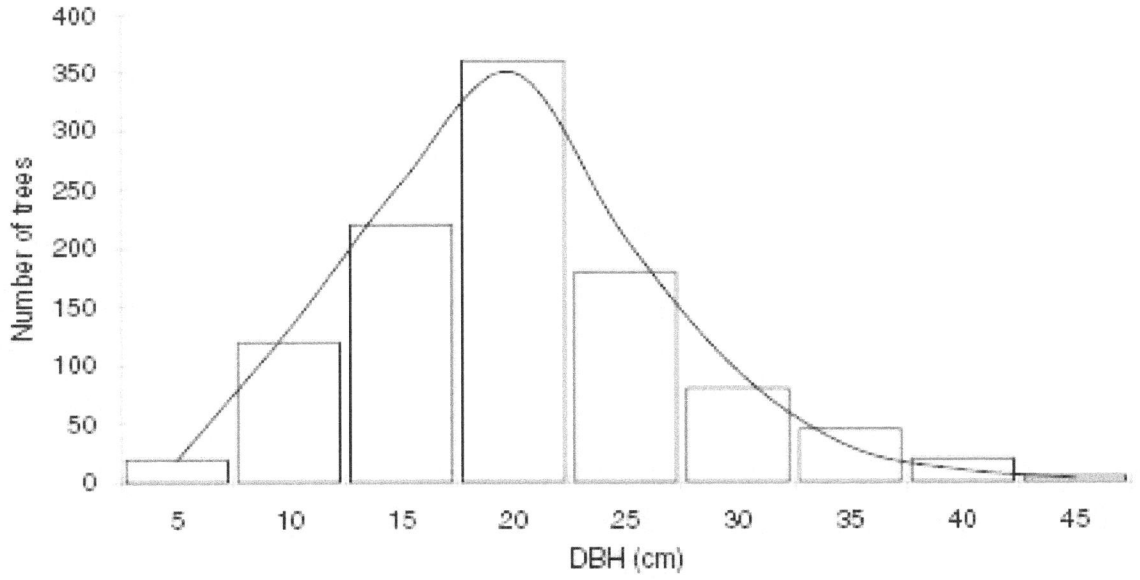

The Authors:

Bernard R. Parresol, Mathematical Statistician, U.S. Department of Agriculture, Forest Service, Southern Research Station, Biometrics Unit, Asheville, NC 28804; **Teresa Fidalgo Fonseca and Carlos Pacheco Marques**, Faculty, Universidade de Trás-os-Montes e Alto Douro, Departamento de Ciências Florestais e Arquitectura Paisagista, Apartado 1013, 5001–801 Vila Real, Portugal.

Cover: Pine stand profile and graphical display of the observed d.b.h. distribution (histogram) and the S_B fitted distribution function (solid line).

June 2010

Southern Research Station
200 W.T. Weaver Blvd.
Asheville, NC 28804

Numerical Details and SAS Programs for Parameter Recovery of the S_B Distribution

Bernard R. Parresol, Teresa Fidalgo Fonseca,
and Carlos Pacheco Marques

Contents

List of Figures

Numerical Details and SAS Programs for Parameter Recovery of the S_B Distribution

Bernard R. Parresol, Teresa Fidalgo Fonseca, and Carlos Pacheco Marques

Abstract

The four-parameter S_B distribution has seen widespread use in growth-and-yield modeling because it covers a broad spectrum of shapes, fitting both positively and negatively skewed data and bimodal configurations. Two recent parameter recovery schemes, an approach whereby characteristics of a statistical distribution are equated with attributes of a stand in order to solve for the parameters of the distribution, are described for the S_B. The first scheme permits recovery of the range and both shape parameters, but the location parameter must be *a priori* specified. The second scheme is an all-parameter recovery model. The details of the parameter recovery models, that is the system of equations with their concomitant constraints, are laid out. A solution technique for the constrained parameter recovery models that uses the Kuhn-Tucker conditions, the Lagrange function, and the Levenberg-Marquardt algorithm is briefly reviewed. Two Statistical Analysis System programs that implement the parameter recovery models, S_B Recovery 3parm and S_B Recovery 4parm, are listed and demonstrated with instructive examples.

Keywords: Basal area-size distribution, constraint functions, diameter distributions, moments, nonlinear programming problem, restricted estimation.

Introduction

Forecasting number of trees in a stand over diameter classes is customarily done through the use of probability density functions (PDF). Many distributions have been utilized such as the beta, Weibull, gamma, and lognormal. Hafley and Schreuder (1977) examined the skewness and kurtosis of various statistical distributions as a measure of the flexibility of the distributions in regard to their changes in shape. They showed that the four-parameter S_B PDF (Johnson 1949, S_B means system bounded) provides greater generality in terms of skewness and kurtosis than many of the usually applied distributions in forestry. Based on Hafley and Schreuder's findings, many growth-and-yield models that used the S_B distribution ensued (e.g., Fonseca 2004, Hafley and Buford 1985, Kamziah and others 1999, Kiviste and others 2003, Lopes 2001, Parresol 2003, Tham 1988, Von Gadow 1983).

A variety of parameter estimation methods are available for the S_B distribution, such as the percentile method, linear and nonlinear regression methods, moments, and maximum likelihood. These have been reviewed and compared by Zhou and McTague (1996) and Kamziah and others (1999). The state-of-the-art approach for parameter estimation in growth-and-yield-modeling is called parameter recovery (Hyink and Moser 1983). Parresol (2003) presented a loblolly pine (*Pinus taeda* L.) growth-and-yield model using the S_B distribution where one parameter of the distribution was fixed and the remaining three parameters were estimated in a parameter-recovery context. Parresol's new methodology was more general than previous S_B-based growth-and yield-models which recovered only one or two parameters (e.g., Newberry and Burk 1985, Parresol 1983, Scolforo and Thiersch 1998). Fonseca (2004) and Fonseca and others (2009) extended Parresol's scheme to create a methodology that completely recovers Johnson's S_B diameter distribution from stand variables. The objectives of this article are (1) to present the details necessary to implement the three-parameter recovery scheme of Parresol (2003) and the all-parameter recovery scheme of Fonseca (2004) and Fonseca and others (2009) and (2) to present and demonstrate the Statistical Analysis System (SAS) programs that employ these schemes.

The S_B Distribution

Let the random variable D represent tree diameter, and let d stand for particular values from the range of D. The equation for Johnson's S_B distribution for tree diameter is

$$f(d) = \begin{cases} \dfrac{\delta\lambda}{\sqrt{2\pi}(d-\xi)(\xi+\lambda-d)}\exp\left\{-\dfrac{1}{2}\left[\gamma+\delta\ln\left(\dfrac{d-\xi}{\xi+\lambda-d}\right)\right]^2\right\}, \\ \quad \xi < d < \xi+\lambda, \delta > 0, -\infty < \gamma < \infty, \lambda > 0, \xi \geq 0 \\ \\ 0 \quad \text{otherwise} \end{cases} \tag{1}$$

It is characterized by the location parameter ξ, the range parameter λ, and shape parameters γ and δ. Although there is no closed form expression for its cumulative distribution function, if $D \sim S_B(\xi, \lambda, \gamma, \delta)$ then

$$z = \gamma + \delta \ln\left[(d - \xi)/(\xi + \lambda - d)\right] \sim \mathcal{N}(0,1) \qquad (2)$$

z being a standard normal deviate. This property means integration of equation (1), i.e., the S_B PDF, over specific classes can be accomplished by application of the well-tabulated standard normal distribution. It is easy to show that the shape of the distribution of D depends only on the parameters γ and δ. For, defining a new variable

$$y = f(d) = (d - \xi)/\lambda \qquad (3)$$

it follows from equation (2) that

$$z_y = \gamma + \delta \ln\left[y/(1 - y)\right] \sim \mathcal{N}(0,1) \qquad (4)$$

and Y must have a distribution of the same shape as D (Johnson and Kotz 1970).

Figure 1 shows a number of the possible shapes that the S_B distribution can assume. Often stands display a unimodal shape in the range of tree diameters, as displayed in figure 1A. The first line is a right or positively skewed shape, which occurs when γ has a positive value. The middle line is a symmetric shape, like a normal curve, which occurs when γ is zero. The third line is a left or negatively skewed shape, which occurs when γ takes on a negative value. Figure 1B shows other shapes that the S_B distribution can assume. Uneven-aged stands typically have a reverse-J shape to the distribution of tree diameters. As seen in the graph, bimodal shapes are possible with the S_B distribution, as might occur with a storm-damaged stand where most of the overstory is taken out but some large trees survive.

Parameter Recovery

The parameter recovery approach uses stand-average attributes such as the mean diameter and basal area per unit area to obtain estimates of the underlying diameter distribution (Hyink and Moser 1983). The fundamental idea is to relate characteristics of an assumed distribution (in our case the S_B), such as percentile points or moments, with attributes of the stand and, thereby, recover the parameters of the distribution that would yield those exact values.

Put another way, in the parameter recovery method, the parameters of the distribution function are solved from a system of equations, equating (measured or predicted) stand attributes to their analytical counterparts (Kangas and Maltamos 2000).

Three-Parameter Recovery System

In Parresol (2003) a parameter recovery model for the range and shape parameters was developed that uses the median and the first and second noncentral moments of

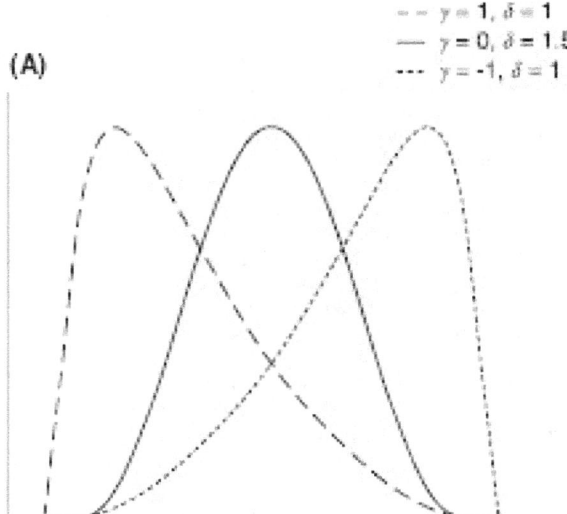

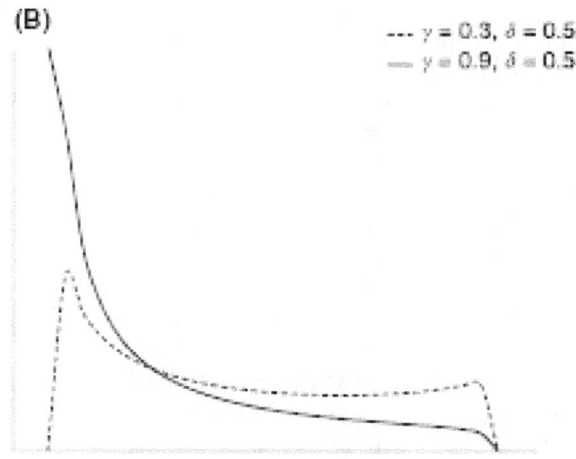

Figure 1—Johnson S_B distributions with various values of the γ and δ shape parameters. (A) displays unimodel shapes (right-skewed for $\gamma = 1$, symmetric for $\gamma = 0$, left-skewed for $\gamma = -1$). (B) displays a reverse-J shaped distribution and a bimodal distribution.

the diameter distribution (average diameter and quadratic mean diameter). The ξ parameter is *a priori* specified. Parresol showed that the γ parameter could be expressed as a function of the other three parameters

$$\gamma = \delta \ln \left[\frac{\lambda}{(d_{median} - \xi)} - 1 \right] \qquad (5)$$

where

d_{median} is the median tree diameter or 50th percentile of the diameter distribution. This allowed for a system of two equations in two unknowns to recover the range and both shape parameters.

$$\bar{d} = \xi + \lambda \mu_1'(y) \qquad (6)$$

$$B = \kappa N \left[\xi^2 + 2\xi\lambda\mu_1'(y) + \lambda^2\mu_2'(y) \right] \qquad (7)$$

where

$\bar{d}$ = average stand diameter
B = basal area per unit area
N = trees per unit area
κ = units conversion ($\pi/40\ 000$ for metric units and $\pi/576$ for English units)
$\mu_1'(y)$ = first noncentral moment of the distribution of Y, and
$\mu_2'(y)$ = second noncentral moment of the distribution of Y

As mentioned, ξ is prespecified. λ and δ are iteratively solved for using equations (6) and (7), and then γ is solved for using equation (5). For details of the derivation of the three-parameter recovery model see Parresol (2003).

All-Parameter Recovery System

Fonseca (2004), working with maritime pine (*P. pinaster* Aiton) diameter distributions, extended the three-parameter recovery scheme to create a methodology that recovers all four parameters of Johnson's S_B distribution from stand variables. In order to recover all the parameters it is necessary to supplement equations (5), (6), and (7) with an additional function. The idea behind parameter recovery is to use values from the statistical distribution that (a) directly relate to stand characteristics, (b) are quantities that foresters can understand, and (c) have a meaningful interpretation. As already stated, the first noncentral moment of statistical distributions is directly related to average stand diameter, and the second noncentral moment is readily understood

as quadratic mean diameter, i.e., the tree of average basal area that we will designate as $d_{\bar{q}}$. A paper by Gove and Patil (1998) gives a meaningful interpretation of the third noncentral moment of statistical distributions as it relates to stand diameter. Specifically, understanding arises when diameter distributions are viewed with respect to tree basal area (basal area-size distribution or BASD) rather than to tree frequency. Designating the BASD mean as d_g, the third noncentral moment of the diameter distribution is the product of the mean BASD and the square of the quadratic mean diameter, that is, $\mu_3'(d) = \bar{d}_g d_{\bar{q}}^2$. Using this property, Fonseca derived the following formula for the S_B distribution:

$$d_g d_{\bar{q}}^2 = \xi^3 + 3\xi^2\lambda\mu_1'(y) + 3\xi\lambda^2\mu_2'(y) + \lambda^3\mu_3'(y) \qquad (8)$$

Inclusion of equation (8) in Parresol's (2003) earlier system allows for the ξ parameter also to be recovered. An estimate of the third noncentral moment of diameter distribution can be calculated from plot diameters as follows:

$$\hat{\mu}_3'(d) = \frac{\sum_{i=1}^{t} d_i^3}{n} \qquad (9)$$

where

n = number of trees on the plot

For details on the development of the all-parameter recovery model please refer to Fonseca (2004) and Fonseca and others (2009).

Procedures for Solving the Parameter Recovery Systems

The S_B parameter recovery strategies involve solving complex systems of nonlinear equations. Parresol's scheme uses two nonlinear equations in two unknowns and Fonseca's scheme is based on three nonlinear equations in three unknowns. By subtracting the left-hand sides of equations (6), (7), and (8) we equate the functions to zero. By squaring the functions we create a system whereby we can use a nonlinear least-squares minimization routine. A least-squares problem is a special form of minimization problem where the objective function (the function to be minimized) is defined as a sum of squares of other functions (in our case nonlinear functions).

$$F(\mathbf{x}) = \frac{1}{2}\left[f_1^2(\mathbf{x}) + \cdots + f_m^2(\mathbf{x}) \right] \qquad (10)$$

where

$\mathbf{x} = (x_1, x_2, \ldots, x_p)$ is a vector of p unknown parameters and $m \geq p$

There are several minimization techniques available to solve for nonlinear systems. The Levenberg-Marquardt (LM) algorithm is one that works well on many practical problems and, thus, is a sensible choice.

Levenberg-Marquardt Algorithm

Starting with an initial value vector x (a guess) to the solution, the LM iterative update formula is (Ralston and Rabinowitz 1978, page 363)

$$\mathbf{x}_{i+1} = \mathbf{x}_i - (\mathbf{J}_i^t \mathbf{J}_i + \theta_i \mathbf{I})^{-1} \mathbf{J}_i^t \mathbf{f}_i \qquad (11)$$

where

$\theta_i \geq 0$ = a scaling factor
$\mathbf{I}$ = an identity matrix, and
the Jacobian at each iteration point x_i is

$$\mathbf{J}_i = \left(\frac{\partial f_j}{\partial x^{(k)}} \right)_{x = x_i} \qquad (12)$$

The Jacobian is a matrix of partial derivatives. For the three-parameter recovery system the partial derivatives are given in Parresol (2003). For the all-parameter recovery system the partial derivatives are given in Fonseca and others (2009). The LM algorithm is a blend of gradient descent (also called steepest descent) and Gauss-Newton iteration. For a detailed explanation of the LM algorithm and its advantages see Ralston and Rabinowitz (1978) and Ranganathan (2004).

Global Minimum, Convergence, and Initial Values

All optimization algorithms converge towards local rather than global optima. The smallest local minimum of an objective function is called the global minimum, and the goal is to find the solution vector that returns the global minimum of the objective function. For the S_B parameter recovery models the absolute minimum of the objective

equation (10) is zero, but the global minimum may be greater than zero due to constraints imposed on the solution. From optimization theory (see Avriel 2003), a local minimizer $\tilde{\mathbf{x}}$ satisfies the following three conditions:

1. There exists a small, feasible neighborhood of $\tilde{\mathbf{x}}$ that does not contain any point x with a smaller function value $F(\mathbf{x}) < F(\tilde{\mathbf{x}})$.

2. The vector of first derivatives (gradient) $\mathbf{g}(\tilde{\mathbf{x}}) = \nabla F(\tilde{\mathbf{x}})$ of the objective function F (projected toward the feasible region) at the point $\tilde{\mathbf{x}}$ is zero.

3. The matrix of second derivatives $\mathbf{G}(\tilde{\mathbf{x}}) = \nabla^2 F(\tilde{\mathbf{x}})$ (Hessian matrix) of the objective function F (projected toward the feasible region) at the point $\tilde{\mathbf{x}}$ is positive definite.

One reason for choosing the LM algorithm is that for $\theta_i > 0$ the inverse matrix in equation (11) always exists and condition 3 is always met. Condition 2 gives us a convenient convergence criterion to stop the iteration of equation (11) and declare that a local minimizer $\tilde{\mathbf{x}}$ has been found. Termination requires the gradient to vanish, or in mathematical terms, that the maximum absolute gradient element be very small, such as

$$\max_j \left| g_j(x^{(k)}) \right| \leq 10^{-5} \qquad (13)$$

Other definitions of convergence can be used. For example, terminate when the Euclidean distance between parameter vectors in consecutive iterations is smaller than a critical value such as 10^{-8}. Multiple tests for convergence are typically used with optimization routines. To check that we are at the global minimum we need to compute the L_1 norm

$$\left\| \mathbf{f}(\tilde{\mathbf{x}}) \right\|_1 = \sum_{i=1}^{m} \left| f_i(\tilde{\mathbf{x}}) \right| \qquad (14)$$

and verify that it is close to zero. It is a good idea to run various optimizations with a pattern of different starting values to check that the global minimum is obtained. If the optimization routine fails, i.e., condition 1 is not met or the maximum number of iterations is exceeded, simply use different starting values.

Initial values are required to start the iteration of equation (11). Normally information from inventory data is available to help guide us in choosing good starting values. We can take the observed minimum and maximum diameters and use their difference as an initial guess for the range parameter λ. For the location parameter ξ, a scaler multiple such as 0.5 to 0.8 of the observed minimum diameter gives a reasonable initial value. Concerning the shape parameter δ, for bimodal shapes use a starting value ≤ 0.7 and for unimodal shapes use an initial value ≥ 1.

Parameter Restrictions

To prevent the LM algorithm [equation (11)] from projecting the parameter vector x into an unfeasible parameter space, it is necessary to impose restrictions on the parameters. Constraints on the parameter space can also prevent unreasonable solutions from occurring. It is important to note that constraints can be equality restrictions or inequality restrictions of the form $\leq$ or $\geq$, but not $<$ or $>$.

Three-parameter recovery system—The constraints are constructed as follows. From equation (5) we know that $\gamma = \delta \ln \left[\lambda / (d_{median} - \xi) - 1 \right]$, and this equation reveals that $\lambda / (d_{median} - \xi) > 1$ to avoid an illegal log argument, thus $d_{median} - \xi < \lambda$. As a practical matter the range should be restricted. A reasonable upper bound is $2 \times$ initial guess for λ. By definition of the S_B distribution, $\delta > 0$. From all this we have

$$d_{median} - \xi < \lambda \leq 2 \times \text{initial } \lambda \text{ value}$$
$$0 < \delta \tag{15}$$

Because constraints must be expressed as $\leq$ or $\geq$, we need to make small adjustments in equation (15). Our final constraints are

$$d_{median} - \xi + 0.01 \leq \lambda \leq 2 \times \text{initial } \lambda \text{ value}$$
$$0.01 \leq \delta \tag{16}$$

All-parameter recovery system—For this system we need both boundary conditions and a linear constraint. In this system ξ is a random parameter. Again, consider the equation $\gamma = \delta \ln \left[\lambda / (d_{median} - \xi) - 1 \right]$. It is obvious that ξ must be less than d_{median} to avoid an illegal log argument. We know that ξ cannot be less than zero, hence $0 \leq \xi < d_{median}$. Alternatively, one can use observed minimum diameter as an upper bound constraint for ξ. The

equation also reveals that $\lambda / (d_{median} - \xi) > 1$ to avoid an illegal log argument, thus $d_{median} - \xi < \lambda$. Because ξ and λ are random parameters, this gives the linear restriction $\xi + \lambda > d_{median}$. As before we want to restrict the range and we know that $\delta > 0$. Gathering all this information gives

$$0 \leq \xi < d_{median}$$
$$\lambda \leq 2 \times \text{initial } \lambda \text{ value}$$
$$0 < \delta \tag{17}$$
$$\xi + \lambda > d_{median}$$

We need to make small adjustments in equation (17) to create the necessary $\leq$ and $\geq$ inequalities. Our final constraints are

$$0 \leq \xi \leq d_{median} - 0.01$$
$$\lambda \leq 2 \times \text{initial } \lambda \text{ value}$$
$$0.01 \leq \delta \tag{18}$$
$$\xi + \lambda \geq d_{median} + 0.01$$

Restricted Estimation

From the previous section we showed that some of the S_B parameters are subject to boundary constraints and that ξ and λ are subject to a linear restriction when recovering all parameters. The Kuhn-Tucker theorem (Avriel 2003, Kuhn and Tucker 1951) is a theorem in nonlinear programming which states that if a regularity condition holds and the objective function F and constraint functions c_i are convex, then a solution $\tilde{x}$ which satisfies the conditions c_i for a vector of multipliers α is a local optimum (a minimum or maximum depending on the problem). The Kuhn-Tucker theorem is a generalization of Lagrange multipliers. The linear combination of objective and constraint functions

$$L(x, \alpha) = F(x) - \sum \alpha_i c_i(x) \tag{19}$$

is the Lagrange function and the coefficients α_i are the Lagrange multipliers. Because of constraints on the parameters in both recovery systems, we will actually minimize the Lagrange function [equation (19)], and the three conditions for a local minimizer $\tilde{x}$ still apply.

Statistical Analysis System Programs

We developed two SAS, version 9.1, programs that utilize the nonlinear programming Levenberg-Marquardt (NLPLM) procedure, part of the interactive matrix language (IML) capabilities of SAS software (SAS Institute Inc. 2004, pages 795–798). The first program, S_B Recovery 3parm, is listed in appendix A. The second program, S_B Recovery 4parm, is given in appendix B. While the two programs share the same structure, there are differences in the input needed, in the makeup of the constraint matrix, and in the system of equations to be solved. Hence, we felt it would be better to create two separate programs rather than one program with dichotomies. It is important to note that the programs can use either the international system of units (the metric system) or the English system of units. For input and output values in the metric system, use the κ-value on line 207 of S_B Recovery 3parm (line 206 should start with an * to make it a comment line) and on line 246 of S_B Recovery 4parm (line 245 should start with an * to make it a comment line). Likewise, for input and output values in the English system, use the κ-value on line 206 of S_B Recovery 3parm (line 207 should start with an * to make it a comment line) and on line 245 of S_B Recovery 4parm (line 246 should start with an * to make it a comment line).

S_B Recovery 3parm

This program is designed to input required data through an Excel® (Microsoft Corporation) file. The file location and name are specified by the user on line 53 of the program (see appendix A). The program checks the validity of the initial values in a "do loop" on lines 254–259. On line 59 the user can supply a descriptive project title that will print on the top of all printed output from the program. The amount of printed output is controlled by the options vector on line 210. The value of the second element of the vector controls the output from the NLPLM procedure. A value of zero turns off output. A value of 1 turns on summaries and iteration history. More output can be generated using values 2–5, but generally the summary and iteration history are more than sufficient. See the SAS/IML® 9.1 "User's Guide" for more information on the options vector (SAS Institute Inc. 2004, pages 343–349). The constraint matrix is initialized on line 238. Lines 261–268 actually set the bounds for λ in the matrix. At the user's discretion, on line 263 a smaller or larger upper bound can be specified for λ, but generally 2 × initial value works well. The

NLPLM procedure gives a return code (RC) that indicates the termination criterion met or the reason for failure. A positive value indicates successful termination, while a negative value indicates unsuccessful termination. An RC = 3 indicates the gradient vanished, that is, convergence as specified by equation (13) was met. An RC = 7 indicates convergence based on Euclidean distance. See the SAS/IML® 9.1 "User's Guide" for explanations of the 20 RC values (SAS Institute Inc. 2004, page 333) and the definitions of the various termination criteria used (pages 349–356). The program creates an output file that contains the label for the observation, the parameter estimates, the value of the L_1 norm [equation (14)], a "YES" or "NO" convergence tag, and the RC from the NLPLM procedure. The length of the label variable is initialized on line 190 and can be set to any length by the user. The program prints the results dataset (line 285), and output is saved to an Excel® file. The file location and name are specified by the user on line 292 of the program.

S_B Recovery 4parm

This program is also designed to input required data through an Excel® file. The file location and name are specified by the user on line 64 of the program (see appendix B). The program checks the validity of the initial values in a "do loop" on lines 308–315. On line 70 the user can supply a descriptive project title that will print on the top of all printed output from the program. As in the first program, the amount of printed output is controlled by the options vector on line 249. Unlike the first program, this program utilizes the TC or termination criteria vector on line 254. This vector permits users to control the maximum number of iterations (first element of the vector) and the maximum number of function calls (second element of the vector). The complexity of solving three simultaneous equations sometimes necessitates increasing these values. The constraint matrix is initialized on lines 291–293. The upper bound constraint for ξ is set on line 317 and for λ on line 319. At the user's discretion, these upper bounds can be changed. Like in the first program, the NLPLM procedure gives a RC that indicates the termination status, and an output file is generated. The length of the label variable is set on line 229. The program prints the results dataset (line 345) and the output is saved to an Excel® file. The file location and name are specified by the user on line 352 of the program.

Examples and Discussion

Practical examples of the S_B recovery SAS programs heretofore described are presented and discussed. The chosen cases were taken from real stands in a selective way in order to provide an overall picture of the programs' implementation and S_B flexibility. In the following examples, stand and tree variable values are expressed in the metric system.

S_B Recovery 3parm

Figure 2 shows an example Excel® input file with variable labels in row 1. ID is stand code (character variable), BA is basal area per unit area (m^2ha^{-1}), and NT is number of trees per unit area (trees ha^{-1}). SBMEDIAN, SBMEAN,

and DMIN refer, respectively, to the median, the average, and the minimum diameter (in cm) of the observed diameter distribution. IV_LAMBDA and IV_DELTA are the initial values set for the λ and the δ parameters. Consider the four observations in figure 2. Let us use this file as input into S_B Recovery 3parm. The Excel® file output by the program is given in figure 3. As we can see, a convergent solution was obtained on all four observations, and the L_1 norm values are very small, $< 10^{-7}$ (essentially zero) for observations "S1104" and "S1606." The use of different starting values resulted in the same solutions confirming that the global minimums were obtained. Recall that we are using restricted estimation and we can see in figure 3 that the $\hat\lambda$ values for "S0204" and "S1906" are at the upper boundary constraint. This is why the L_1 norm values are slightly positive. However, they are sufficiently small as not to cause concern.

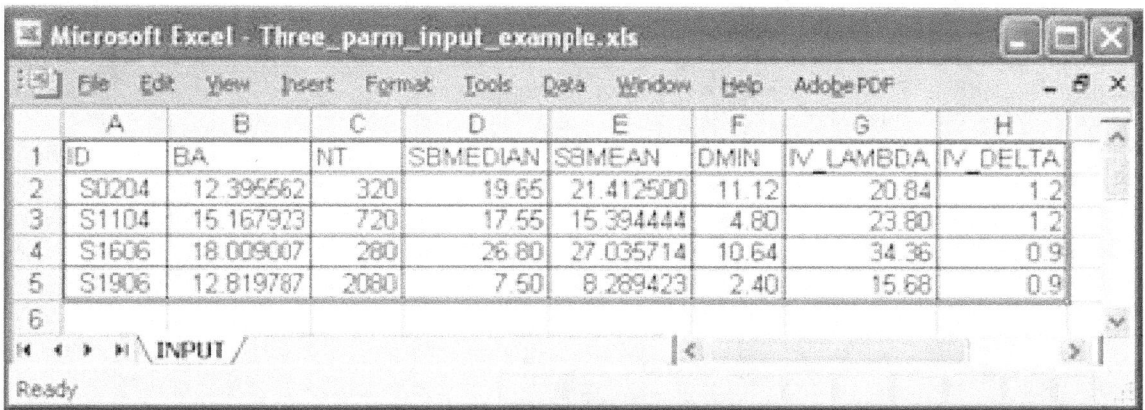

Figure 2—Input file used on S_B Recovery 3parm program (see text for variable labels description).

	A	B	C	D	E	F	G	H
1	ID	BA	NT	SBMEDIAN	SBMEAN	DMIN	IV_LAMBDA	IV_DELTA
2	S0204	12.395562	320	19.65	21.412500	11.12	20.84	1.2
3	S1104	15.167923	720	17.55	15.394444	4.80	23.80	1.2
4	S1606	18.009007	280	26.80	27.035714	10.64	34.36	0.9
5	S1906	12.819787	2080	7.50	8.289423	2.40	15.68	0.9

Figure 3—Output file created by S_B Recovery 3parm program.

	A	B	C	D	E	F	G	H
1	LABEL	XI	LAMBDA	GAMMA	DELTA	L1NORM	CONVERGE	RC
2	S0204	11.12	41.67000	1.36842	1.00831	0.267617	YES	3
3	S1104	4.80	16.35537	-0.44579	0.35293	1.97E-08	YES	3
4	S1606	10.64	33.85450	0.05795	0.63881	9.50E-09	YES	3
5	S1906	2.40	31.35000	2.23179	1.36216	0.094095	YES	6

Hence, there is no need to change the upper bound for λ for these two observations.

A δ value < 0.7 generally results in a bimodal shape. For observation "S1104" we have $\delta = 0.35$ and $\gamma = -0.45$ which should give a decidedly left-skewed bimodal shape, and for observation "S1606" we have $\delta = 0.64$ and $\gamma = 0.06$ which should give a slightly right-skewed bimodal shape. The observed and S_B simulated frequencies by 5-cm diameter classes are shown in figure 4. In part A, for observation "S0204," we have a classic right-skewed unimodal graph. We see in part B (observation "S1104") a mode at 10 cm and the second much larger mode (as expected) at 20 cm. There is a perfect pairing of the observed and simulated mode locations and the S_B curve gives a good fit to the observed mode heights. Part C of the graph displays another bimodal distribution (observation "S1606") with predicted modes at 15 and 40 cm. The observed modes occurred at 20 and 40 cm, and though there is some disagreement, the S_B curve is a reasonable simulation. Statistical distributions such as the Weibull and lognormal cannot fit such shapes. Finally, in part D (observation "S1906"), we see a very good match between the observed and predicted reverse-J shaped distributions.

S_B Recovery 4parm

Let us look at new examples using the all-parameter recovery system. We will use as input into program S_B Recovery 4parm the file displayed in figure 5. The additional variable used as input, labeled SBMUPRIME3, refers to the third noncentral moment of diameter distribution. The variable IV_XI is the initial value for the ξ parameter (in our case it was set to 0.8 of observed minimum diameter). The Excel® file output by the program is given in figure 6. There are several things to note in the output file. Observation "S2112" had an unsuccessful termination, the RC = -8 code means maximum number of iterations exceeded. For observation "S2504" the solution for δ occurred on the lower boundary at 0.01. Figure 7 is a graph of "S2504" and illustrates that this is not a reasonable simulation. The solution for observation "S2804" looks good. Notice that the ξ value is at its lower boundary of zero but the L_1 norm is very small. The solution for observation "S0406" looks reasonable but has the largest L_1 norm value of the four solutions. This is probably due to the value of λ being at its upper bound.

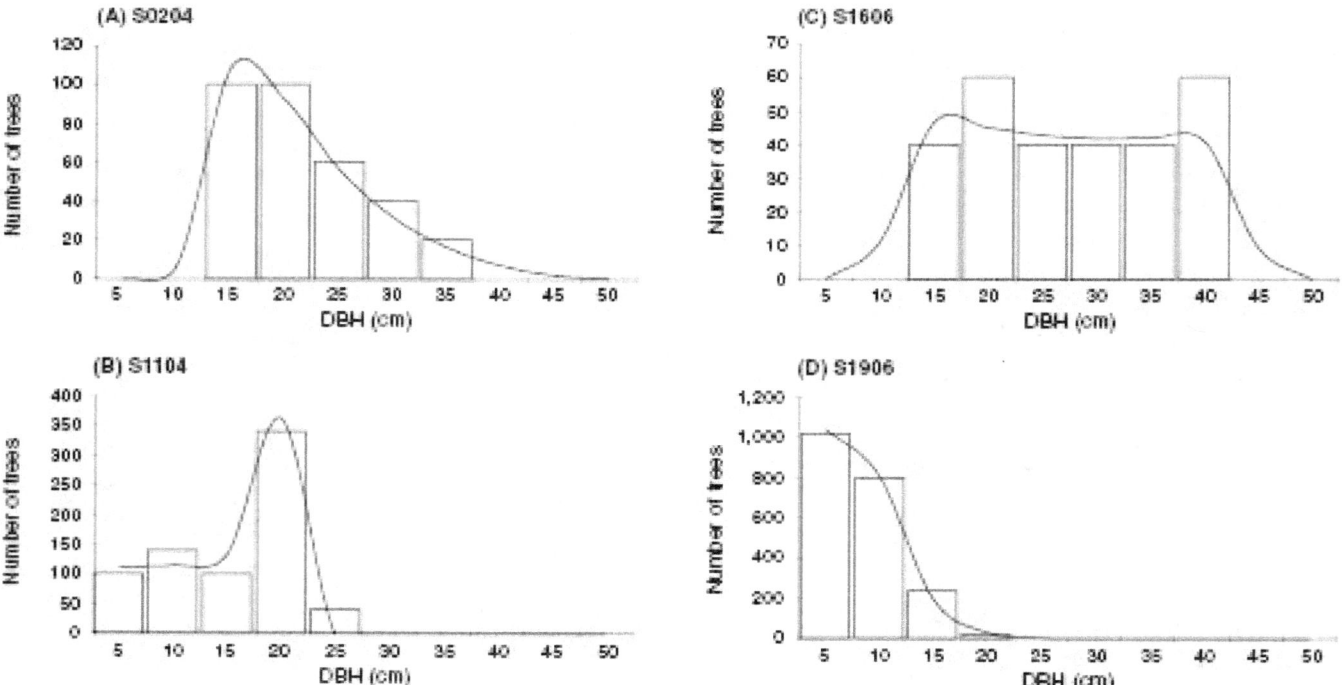

Figure 4—Observed frequencies and S_B simulated distributions using the three-parameter recovery program. (A) Observation "S0204" is a classic right-skewed unimodal fit. In (B) observation "S1104" and (C) observation "S1606" we see reasonable bimodal fits to the observed frequencies. (D) observation "S1906" shows an excellent fit to the reverse-J shaped distribution.

Microsoft Excel - Four_parm_input_example.xls

File　Edit　View　Insert　Format　Tools　Data　Window　Help　Adobe PDF

	A	B	C	D	E	F	G	H	I
1	ID	BA	NT	SBMEDIAN	SBMEAN	SBMUPRIME3	IV_XI	IV_LAMBDA	IV_DELTA
2	S2112	39.398713	520	29.60	30.669231	31115.6217692	18.56	25.74	1.2
3	S2504	44.859634	1200	21.75	21.255000	11149.8915500	10.00	20.00	0.5
4	S2804	38.357857	920	22.65	22.680435	12789.9818913	3.00	35.00	2.5
5	S0406	37.391770	1900	14.90	15.408421	4284.6042105	6.72	21.58	1.8
6									

⏮ ◀ ▶ ⏭ \INPUT/

Ready

Figure 5—Input file used on S_B Recovery 4parm program (see text for variable labels description).

Microsoft Excel - Four_parm_output_example.xls

File　Edit　View　Insert　Format　Tools　Data　Window　Help　Adobe PDF

	A	B	C	D	E	F	G	H
1	LABEL	XI	LAMBDA	GAMMA	DELTA	L1NORM	CONVERGE	RC
2	S2112	25.33575	11.24027	0.06782	0.13779	0.015456	NO	-8
3	S2504	16.27094	9.94624	-0.00204	0.01	0.004346	YES	3
4	S2804	0	47.33625	0.24323	2.82539	0.000732	YES	3
5	S0406	6.83758	43.16000	2.81293	1.91237	0.032907	YES	3
6								

⏮ ◀ ▶ ⏭ \OUTPUT/

Ready

Figure 6—Output file created by S_B Recovery 4parm program.

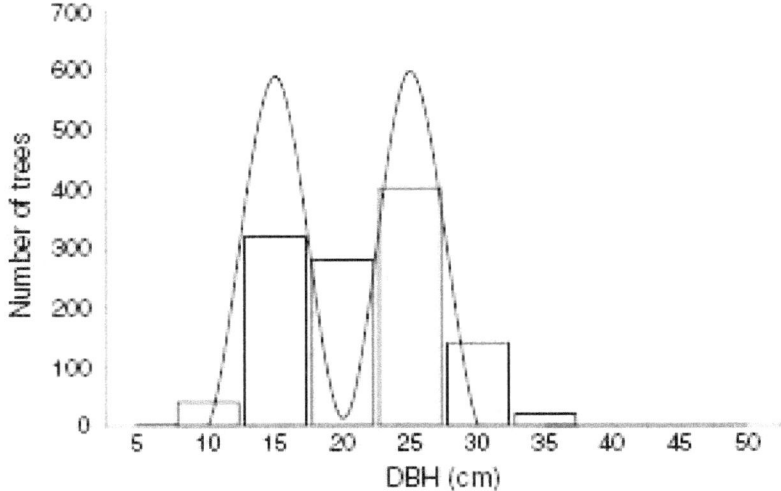

Figure 7—Observed frequencies and S_B simulated distribution for observation "S2504" using the initial solution of the all-parameter recovery program.

Let us do another run of the program. The $\hat{\xi} = 16.27$ cm solution for observation "S2504" seems quite large so we will impose the observed plot minimum diameter of 12 cm as an upper bound. Line 318 of the program is a blank spacing line. To change the upper bound ξ constraint for observation "S2504" we add the following "IF" statement on line 318: "IF LABEL='S2504' THEN UB_XI = 12." For observations "S2112" and "S0406" we will try a different set of starting values. The updated input file is shown in figure 8. The output file from this new run is shown in figure 9. We see that this time a convergent solution was obtained on "S2112" and the L_1 norm goes to zero. The λ and δ values have substantially increased and are more in line with expectations. Figure 10A shows a good correspondence between the observed and simulated distributions. The new solution for observation "S2504" has a larger L_1 norm (due to the new ξ constraint), but compare the graph based on the old solution displayed in figure 7 with the new graph shown in figure 10B. It is obvious that the new solution, based on imposing observed minimum diameter as an upper bound constraint on ξ, gives a superior fit against the observed distribution. Concerning observation

"S2804" figure 10C indicates a close conformance between the observed and predicted distribution. For observation "S0406," looking at the old L_1 norm value in figure 6 (≈ 0.03) and the new L_1 norm value in figure 9 (≈ 0), we see the original convergent solution was at a local minimum. The new solution is at the global minimum and is displayed in figure 10D.

As a final example, let us refit observation "S1104" using the all-parameter recovery program. The input for this observation was shown in figure 2 as input for S_B Recovery 3parm. We need to include the value for SBMUPRIME3 which is 5014.2784444. The solution is as follows: $\hat{\xi} = 6.47538$, $\hat{\lambda} = 14.68004$, $\hat{\gamma} = 0.30239$, $\hat{\delta} = 0.26946$, and the L_1 norm $= 1.83 \times 10^{-12}$. The observed and simulated distributions are shown in figure 11. Compared to figure 4B, we see a much closer correspondence between observed and predicted frequencies in the 10- and 15-cm diameter classes. In this instance, the all-parameter recovery solution provides a better fit compared to the three-parameter recovery solution.

	A	B	C	D	E	F	G	H	I
1	ID	BA	NT	SBMEDIAN	SBMEAN	SBMUPRIME3	IV_XI	IV_LAMBDA	IV_DELTA
2	S2112	39.398713	520	29.60	30.669231	31115.6217692	18.56	25.74	0.8
3	S2504	44.859634	1200	21.75	21.255000	11149.8915600	10.00	20.00	0.5
4	S2804	38.357857	920	22.65	22.680435	12789.9818913	3.00	35.00	2.5
5	S0406	37.391770	1900	14.90	15.408421	4284.6042105	6.72	21.58	1

Figure 8—Updated initial values used on S_B Recovery 4parm program (see text for details).

	A	B	C	D	E	F	G	H
1	LABEL	XI	LAMBDA	GAMMA	DELTA	L1NORM	CONVERGE	RC
2	S2112	24.39041	16.06021	0.36354	0.49547	3.64E-12	YES	3
3	S2504	12	16.66871	-0.18498	0.53924	0.028909	YES	3
4	S2804	0	47.33625	0.24323	2.82539	0.000732	YES	3
5	S0406	9.66245	14.40509	0.40168	0.71752	4.29E-10	YES	3

Figure 9—Output file created by S_B Recovery 4parm program for the new run with updated initial values.

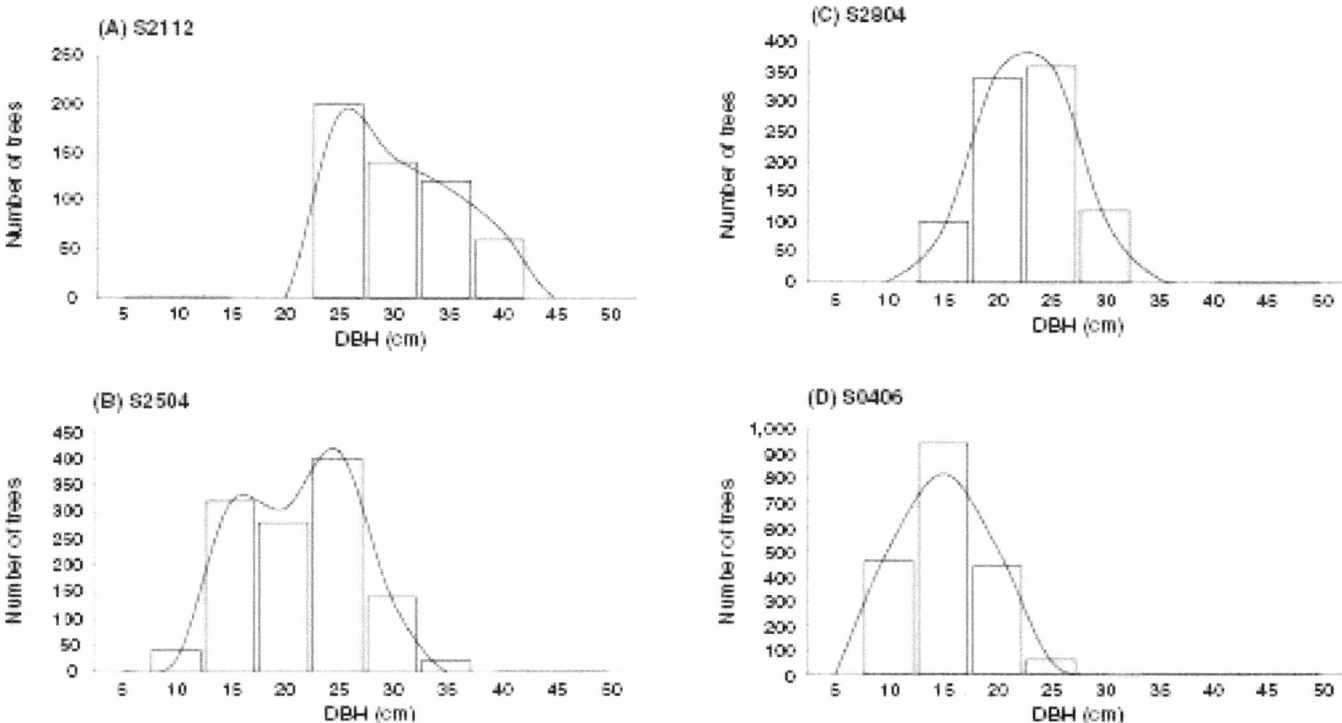

Figure 10—Observed frequencies and S_B simulated distributions using the updated output values of the all-parameter recovery program. All four graphs (A-D) display good fits to the observed frequencies.

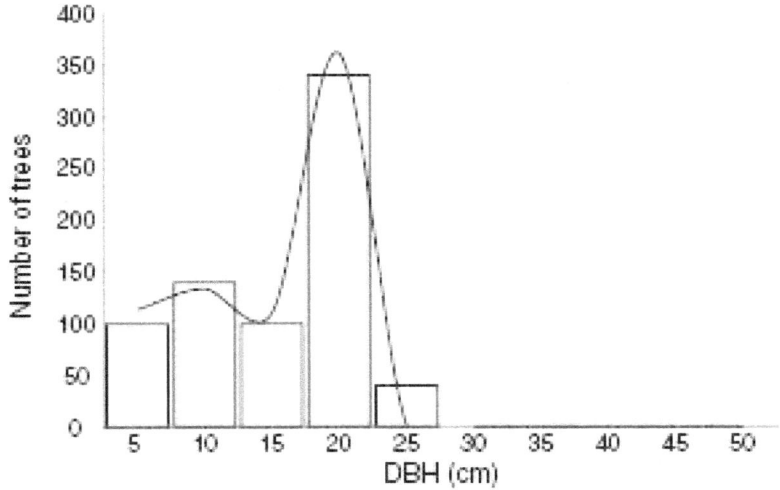

Figure 11—Observed frequencies and S_B simulated distribution for observation "S1104" using the all-parameter recovery program.

Concluding Remarks

Distinct parameter estimation methods are available for the S_B distribution. Nevertheless, at the state-of-the-art, few studies have been conducted for its inclusion in stand models through a moment recovery-based approach. A major reason is that the S_B parameter recovery strategies involve solving complex systems of nonlinear equations. In this paper we presented methodology that was implemented in two SAS programs: S_B Recovery 3parm and S_B Recovery 4parm.

The programs were designed using a robust nonlinear least-squares minimization technique, the LM algorithm, and exploitation of the IML capabilities of SAS software. It is necessary to impose restrictions on the parameters to prevent projecting the parameters into an unfeasible space and/or to avoid unreasonable solutions. Restricted estimation was achieved using the Kuhn-Tucker theorem and the Lagrange function.

Instructive examples of the S_B recovery models were presented in order to illustrate their use. Users should be capable of reproducing the example runs and doing new simulations in an easy manner. SAS programs in text files are available by request from the authors.

Acknowledgments

This study was funded by the Forest Service, Southern Research Station, and Instituto Nacional de Investigação Agrária e das Pescas (under project POAgro 372). We extend special thanks to KaDonna Randolph and Bill Smith for their critical reviews and valuable suggestions.

Literature Cited

Avriel, M. 2003. Nonlinear programming: analysis and methods. Mineola, NY: Dover Publications. 512 p.

Fonseca, T.F. 2004. Modelação do crescimento, mortalidade e distribuição diamétrica, do pinhal bravo no Vale do Tâmega. Vila Real, Portugal: Universidade de Trás-os-Montes e Alto Douro. 248 p. Ph.D. dissertation. In Portugese.

Fonseca, T.F.; Marques, C.P.; Parresol, B.R. 2009. Describing maritime pine diameter distributions with Johnson's S_B distribution using a new all-parameter recovery approach. Forest Science. 55(4): 367–373.

Gove, J.H.; Patil, G.P. 1998. Modeling the basal area-size distribution of forest stands: a compatible approach. Forest Science. 44(2): 285–297.

Hafley, W.L.; Buford, M.A. 1985. A bivariate model for growth and yield prediction. Forest Science. 31(1): 237–247.

Hafley, W.L.; Schreuder, H.T. 1977. Statistical distributions for fitting diameter and height data in even-aged stands. Canadian Journal of Forest Research. 7: 481–487.

Hyink, D.M.; Moser, J.W., Jr. 1983. A generalized framework for projecting forest yield and stand structure using diameter distributions. Forest Science. 29(1): 85–95.

Johnson, N.L. 1949. Systems of frequency curves generated by methods of translation. Biometrika. 36: 149–176.

Johnson, N.L.; Kotz, S. 1970. Continuous univariate distributions-1. New York: John Wiley. 300 p.

Karnziah, A.K.; Ahmad, M.I.; Lapongan, J. 1999. Nonlinear regression approach to estimating Johnson S_B parameters for diameter data. Canadian Journal of Forest Research. 29: 310–314.

Kangas, A.; Maltamo, M. 2000. Calibrating predicted diameter distribution with additional information. Forest Science. 46: 390–396.

Kiviste, A.; Nilson, A.; Hordo, M.; Merenäkk, M. 2003. Diameter distribution models and height-diameter equations for Estonian forests. In: Amaro, A.; Reed, D.; Soares, P., eds. Modelling forest systems. Wallingford, UK: CABI Publishing: 169–179. Chapter 15.

Kuhn, H.W.; Tucker, A.W. 1951. Nonlinear programming. In: Proceedings, 2^d Berkeley symposium on mathematical statistics and probability. Berkeley, CA: University of California Press: 481–492.

Lopes, S. 2001. Modelação matemática da distribuição de diâmetros em povoamentos de pinheiro bravo. Coimbra, Portugal: Universidade de Coimbra. 102 p. M.S. thesis. In Portugese.

Newbury, J.D.; Burk, T.E. 1985. S_B distribution-based models for individual tree merchantable volume-total volume ratio. Forest Science. 31: 389–398.

Parresol, B.R. 1983. Modeling diameter distributions in southern pine plantations. SP-83-075. Baton Rouge, LA: Louisiana State University. 49 p. Masters of Applied Statistics special problem.

Parresol, B.R. 2003. Recovering parameters of Johnson's S_B distribution. Res. Pap. SRS–31. Asheville, NC: U.S. Department of Agriculture Forest Service, Southern Research Station. 9 p.

Ralston, A.; Rabinowitz, P. 1978. A first course in numerical analysis. 2^d ed. New York: McGraw-Hill. 556 p.

Ranganathan, A. 2004. The Levenberg-Marquardt algorithm. http://www.cc.gatech.edu/~ananth/docs/lmtut.pdf. [Date accessed: June 22, 2009].

SAS Institute Inc. 2004. SAS/IML® 9.1 user's guide. Cary, NC: SAS Institute Inc. 1,040 p.

Scolforo, J.R.S.; Thierschi, A. 1998. Estimativas e testes da distribuição de frequência diamétrica para *Eucalyptus camaldulensis*, através da distribuição S_B, por diferentes métodos de ajuste. Scientia Forestalis. 54: 93–106. In Portugese.

Tham, Å. 1988. Estimate and test frequency distributions with the Johnson S_B function from stand parameters in young mixed stands after different thinning treatments. In: Ek, A.R.; Shifley, S.R.; Burk, T.E., eds. Forest growth modelling and prediction. Proceedings of the IUFRO conference. Gen. Tech. Rep. NC–120. St. Paul, MN: U.S. Department of Agriculture Forest Service, North Central Forest Experiment Station: 255–262. Vol. 1.

Von Gadow, K. 1983. Fitting distributions in *Pinus patula* stands. Suid-Afrikaanse Bosboutydskrif. 126: 20–29.

Zhou, B.; McTague, J.P. 1996. Comparison and evaluation of five methods of estimation of the Johnson system of parameters. Canadian Journal of Forest Research. 26: 928–935.

Appendix A

SAS Source Code for S_B Recovery 3parm

(Note: Line numbers are for reference and are not part of the program.)

```
1  /******************************************************************************/
2  /*                                                                          */
3  /*                  PROGRAM SB RECOVERY 3PARM (SAS version 9.1)             */
4  /*                                                                          */
5  /*   DESIGNED FOR TREE DIAMETER DISTRIBUTIONS, THIS PROGRAM USES A          */
6  /*   PERCENTILE-MOMENT METHOD TO RECOVER THE RANGE PARAMETER                */
7  /*   (LAMBDA) AND BOTH SHAPE PARAMETERS (GAMMA, DELTA) OF JOHNSON'S         */
8  /*   SB DISTRIBUTION. THE LOCATION PARAMETER (XI) AND INITIAL               */
9  /*   VALUES FOR LAMBDA AND DELTA MUST BE SUPPLIED TO START THE              */
10 /*   ITERATIVE LEVENBERG-MARQUARDT PROCEDURE.                               */
11 /*                                                                          */
12 /*   INPUT VARIABLES:                                                       */
13 /*                                                                          */
14 /*   ID = IDENTIFICATION CHARACTER VARIABLE FOR LABELING PURPOSES           */
15 /*   BA = STAND BASAL AREA PER UNIT AREA                                    */
16 /*   NT = NUMBER OF TREES PER UNIT AREA                                     */
17 /*   SBMEDIAN  = MEDIAN DIAMETER                                            */
18 /*   SBMEAN    = AVERAGE DIAMETER                                           */
19 /*   DMIN      = MINIMUM DIAMETER, RECODED AS XI IN THE PROGRAM             */
20 /*   IV_LAMBDA = INITIAL OR STARTING VALUE FOR LAMBDA                       */
21 /*   IV_DELTA  = INITIAL OR STARTING VALUE FOR DELTA                        */
22 /*                                                                          */
23 /*   OUTPUT VARIABLES:                                                      */
24 /*                                                                          */
25 /*   LABEL  = IDENTIFICATION CHARACTER VARIABLE                             */
26 /*   XI     = LOCATION PARAMETER                                            */
27 /*   LAMBDA = RANGE PARAMETER                                               */
28 /*   GAMMA  = SHAPE PARAMETER RELATED TO SKEWNESS                           */
29 /*   DELTA  = SHAPE PARAMETER                                               */
30 /*   L1_NORM = VALUE OF L1 NORM OF THE MINIMIZED FUNCTIONS                  */
31 /*   CONVERGE = 'YES' OR 'NO' CHARACTER VARIABLE FOR CONVERGENCE            */
32 /*   RC = SAS RETURN CODE FROM IML ROUTINE NLPLM INDICATING WHICH           */
33 /*        CONVERGENCE CRITERIA WAS MET OR REASON FOR NONCONVERGENCE         */
34 /*                                                                          */
35 /*   Reference:   Parresol, B.R. 2003. Recovering parameters of            */
36 /*               Johnson's SB distribution. USDA Forest Service             */
37 /*               Research Paper SRS-31. 9 p.                                */
38 /*                                                                          */
39 /*   Programmed by Bernard R. Parresol                                      */
40 /*               USDA Forest Service                                        */
41 /*               Southern Research Station                                  */
42 /*               200 WT Weaver Boulevard                                    */
43 /*               Asheville, NC 28804  USA                                   */
44 /*                                                                          */
45 /******************************************************************************/
46
47 OPTIONS NODATE SOURCE;
48
49 *-----     READ DATA FROM AN EXCEL FILE;
50 *-----     USER SUPPLIED DATAFILE IN PROC IMPORT;
51
52 PROC IMPORT OUT= WORK.ONE
53              DATAFILE= "filename"
54              DBMS=EXCEL REPLACE;
55      GETNAMES=YES;
56 RUN;
57
58 TITLE '3 PARAMETER RECOVERY SYSTEM FOR SB DISTRIBUTION';
59 * TITLE2 '-xxxxxxxxxx-';   /* <-- USER CAN ADD DESCRIPTIVE PROJECT TITLE */
60
```

```
61  PROC IML;   /* START MATRIX LANGUAGE */
62
63  START FCN(X)
64  GLOBAL(K,C,i,BA,NT,SBMEDIAN,SBMEAN,XI,LAMBDA,DELTA,GAMMA,R,DM1,DM2,F);
65
66  /***********************************************************/
67  /*                                                         */
68  /*      MODULE FCN IS CALLED BY PROCEDURE NLPLM TO         */
69  /*      EVALUATE THE LEFT-HAND SIDE OF EQUATIONS:          */
70  /*          FCN(LAMBDA,DELTA) - SBMEAN = 0                 */
71  /*          FCN(LAMBDA,DELTA) - BA     = 0                 */
72  /*                                                         */
73  /***********************************************************/
74
75  *-----     SOLVE FOR GAMMA GIVEN ESTIMATES OF XI, LAMBDA, AND DELTA;
76
77          LAMBDA = X[1];
78          DELTA  = X[2];
79          GAMMA  = DELTA*LOG(LAMBDA/(SBMEDIAN[i]-XI)-1);
80
81  *-----     OBTAIN MOMENTS OF SB DISTRIBUTION;
82
83          A = {.M .P};                 /* LIMITS OF INTEGRATION   */
84          R = 1;                       /* EXPONENT FOR 1ST MOMENT */
85          CALL QUAD(DM,"MOMENT",A)     /* NUMERICAL INTEGRATION   */
86              EPS=1E-10;
87          DM1 = C*DM;                  /* VALUE OF FIRST MOMENT   */
88
89          R = 2;                       /* EXPONENT FOR 2ND MOMENT */
90          CALL QUAD(DM,"MOMENT",A)     /* NUMERICAL INTEGRATION   */
91              EPS=1E-10;
92          DM2 = C*DM;                  /* VALUE OF SECOND MOMENT  */
93
94  *-----     COMPUTE VALUES OF FCN;
95
96          F = {0 0};
97          F[1] = XI + LAMBDA*DM1 - SBMEAN[i];
98          F[2] = (XI**2 + 2*XI*LAMBDA*DM1 + LAMBDA**2*DM2)*K*NT[i] - BA[i];
99          RETURN(F);
100 FINISH FCN;
101
102
103 START MOMENT(Z) GLOBAL(DELTA,GAMMA,R);
104
105 /***********************************************************/
106 /*                                                         */
107 /*      MODULE MOMENT IS FOR EVALUATING THE                */
108 /*      MOMENTS OF THE SB DISTRIBUTION.                    */
109 /*                                                         */
110 /***********************************************************/
111
112   V = EXP(-.5*Z**2)/(1 + EXP((GAMMA-Z)/DELTA))**R;
113   RETURN(V);
114 FINISH MOMENT;
115
116
```

```
117 START PSEUDO(Z) GLOBAL(DELTA,GAMMA,R);
118
119 /*********************************************/
120 /*                                           */
121 /*    MODULE PSEUDO IS FOR EVALUATING THE    */
122 /*    PSEUDO-MOMENTS OF THE SB DISTRIBUTION. */
123 /*                                           */
124 /*********************************************/
125
126   V = Z*EXP(-.5*Z**2)/(1 + EXP((GAMMA-Z)/DELTA))**R;
127   RETURN(V);
128 FINISH PSEUDO;
129
130
131 START DERIV(X) GLOBAL(K,C,i,XI,LAMBDA,GAMMA,DELTA,R,DM1,DM2,SBMEDIAN,NT);
132
133 /*********************************************/
134 /*                                           */
135 /*    MODULE DERIV IS CALLED BY NLPLM        */
136 /*    TO EVALUATE THE PARTIAL DERIVATIVES OF */
137 /*        FCN(LAMBDA,DELTA) = SBMEAN         */
138 /*        FCN(LAMBDA,DELTA) = BA             */
139 /*                                           */
140 /*********************************************/
141
142 *-----    OBTAIN THIRD MOMENT;
143
144       A = {.M .P};                /* LIMITS OF INTEGRATION    */
145       R = 3;                      /* EXPONENT FOR 3RD MOMENT  */
146       CALL QUAD(DM,"MOMENT",A)    /* NUMERICAL INTEGRATION    */
147         EPS=1E-10 PEAK=1 SCALE=0.1;
148       DM3 = C*DM;                 /* VALUE OF THIRD MOMENT    */
149
150 *-----    OBTAIN PSEUDO-MOMENTS;
151
152       R = 1;                      /* EXPONENT FOR 1ST PSEUDO-MOMENT */
153       CALL QUAD(PM,"PSEUDO",A)    /* NUMERICAL INTEGRATION          */
154         EPS=1E-10 PEAK=1 SCALE=0.1;
155       PM1 = C*PM;                 /* VALUE OF FIRST PSEUDO-MOMENT   */
156
157       R = 2;                      /* EXPONENT FOR 2ND PSEUDO-MOMENT */
158       CALL QUAD(PM,"PSEUDO",A)    /* NUMERICAL INTEGRATION          */
159         EPS=1E-10 PEAK=1 SCALE=0.1;
160       PM2 = C*PM;                 /* VALUE OF SECOND PSEUDO-MOMENT  */
161
162       R = 3;                      /* EXPONENT FOR 3RD PSEUDO-MOMENT */
163       CALL QUAD(PM,"PSEUDO",A)    /* NUMERICAL INTEGRATION          */
164         EPS=1E-10 PEAK=1 SCALE=0.1;
165       PM3 = C*PM;                 /* VALUE OF THIRD PSEUDO-MOMENT   */
166
167 *-----    DEFINE COMMON ELEMENTS OF DERIVATIVES;
168
169       DM2_1 = DM2 - DM1;
170       DM3_2 = DM3 - DM2;
171       PM2_1 = PM2 - PM1;
172       PM3_2 = PM3 - PM2;
173       DN = LAMBDA - SBMEDIAN[i] + XI;
174
175 *-----    COMPUTE JACOBIAN MATRIX;
176
```

```
177            J = J(2,2,0);
178            J[1,1] = DM1 + LAMBDA * DM2_1 / DN;                      /* f1/LAMBDA */
179            J[1,2] = LAMBDA*PM2_1 / (DELTA*DELTA);                   /* f1/DELTA  */
180            J[2,1] = (XI*DM1 + LAMBDA*DM2 + (XI*LAMBDA
181                     *DM2_1 + LAMBDA**2*DM3_2) / DN)*2*K*NT[i];       /* f2/LAMBDA */
182            J[2,2] = LAMBDA/DELTA**2*(XI*PM2_1 + LAMBDA*PM3_2)
183                     *2*K*NT[i];                                      /* f2/DELTA  */
184         RETURN (J);
185 FINISH DERIV;
186
187
188 ***********  ------->  EXECUTE PROGRAM  <------  ***************;
189
190     LABEL = '12345';          /* TO LABEL OUTPUT, LENGTH CAN BE SET BY USER */
191 CONVERGE = '123';             /* INITIALIZE CHARACTER VARIABLE OF LENGTH 3  */
192
193 *------   SET UP OUTPUT DATASET TO HOLD PARAMETER ESTIMATES AND RESULTS;
194
195 CREATE RESULTS VAR {LABEL XI LAMBDA GAMMA DELTA L1_NORM CONVERGE RC};
196
197 USE ONE;                      /* INPUT DATASET USED BY PROC IML */
198 READ ALL VAR{IO BA NT SBMEDIAN SBMEAN DMIN IV_LAMBDA IV_DELTA};
199
200 NOBS = NROW(BA);                      /* NUMBER OF OBSERVATIONS */
201 IV = IV_LAMBDA||IV_DELTA;             /* MATRIX CONTAINING INITAL VALUES */
202
203 *------   INITIALIZATION;
204
205   PI = 4*ATAN(1);
206 *--K = PI/576;                 /* CONVERSION TO ft² - USE FOR ENGLISH SYSTEM  */
207    K = PI/40000;              /* CONVERSION TO m²  - USE FOR METRIC SYSTEM   */
208    C = 1/SQRT(2*PI);          /* CONSTANT FOR MOMENTS                        */
209
210   OPTN = {2 1};               /* OPTIONS VECTOR                              */
211                               /* 1ST VALUE IS NUMBER OF EQUATIONS IN SYSTEM  */
212                               /* 2ND VALUE DETERMINES AMOUNT OF PRINTED OUTPUT */
213                               /* 0=NO OUTPUT, 1=SUMMARIES & ITERATION HISTORY */
214
215
216 /*---  BOUNDARY CONDITIONS ARE IMPOSED WITH THE CON OR CONSTRAINTS    ---*/
217 /*---  MATRIX. CONSTRAINTS MUST USE >= AND <= INEQUALITIES, NOT > OR < ---*/
218 /*---  INEQUALITIES. WITH THIS IN MIND, WE USE THE FOLLOWING FACTS TO ---*/
219 /*---  CONSTRUCT THE NECESSARY CON MATRIX. GAMMA (G) IS A FUNCTION OF ---*/
220 /*---  THE OTHER 3 PARAMETERS XI, LAMBDA(L) AND DELTA (D) PLUS THE    ---*/
221 /*---  MEDIAN DIAMETER (SBMEDIAN), i.e. G = D*LN(L/(SBMEDIAN-XI)-1).  ---*/
222 /*---  THE EQUATION REVEALS THAT L/(SBMEDIAN-XI) > 1 TO AVOID AN      ---*/
223 /*---  ILLEGAL LOG ARGUMENT, THUS SBMEDIAN-XI < L. AS A PRACTICAL     ---*/
224 /*---  MATTER THE RANGE SHOULD BE RESTRICTED. A REASONABLE UPPER BOUND ---*/
225 /*---  IS 2xINITIAL GUESS FOR L. BY DEFINITION OF THE SB DISTRIBUTION, ---*/
226 /*---  D > 0. GATHERING ALL THIS TOGETHER, WE HAVE:                   ---*/
227 /*---                                                                 ---*/
228 /*---       SBMEDIAN-XI < L <= 2 x IV_L   (IV IS INITIAL VALUE)       ---*/
229 /*---            0 < D                                                ---*/
230 /*---                                                                 ---*/
231 /*---  BECAUSE CONSTRAINTS MUST BE EXPRESSED AS <= OR >=, WE NEED TO  ---*/
232 /*---  MAKE SMALL ADJUSTMENTS. OUR FINAL CONSTRAINTS ARE:            ---*/
233 /*---                                                                 ---*/
234 /*---       SBMEDIAN-XI+0.01 <= L <= 2 x IV_L                        ---*/
235 /*---            0.01 <= D                                            ---*/
236
```

```
237
238   CON = {0 1E-2, 100 .};      /* INITIALIZE PARAMETER CONSTRAINTS MATRIX */
239                               /* ELEMENTS OF ROW 1 ARE LOWER BOUNDS FOR  */
240                               /* LAMBDA & DELTA. ELEMENTS OF ROW 2 ARE   */
241                               /* UPPER BOUNDS FOR LAMBDA & DELTA. A '.'   */
242                               /* OR MISSING VALUE MEANS NO BOUNDARY.      */
243
244   *-----    PROCESS OBSERVATIONS;
245
246   DO i = 1 TO NOBS;           /* LOOP THROUGH OBSERVATIONS */
247
248      LABEL = ID[i];
249      XI=DMIN[i];
250      x=IV[i,];               /* INITAL VALUES VECTOR FOR PARAMETERS  */
251
252   *-----    CHECK VALIDITY OF INITIAL VALUES;
253
254      IF x[1] < SBMEDIAN[i]-XI+0.01 | x[2] < 0.01 THEN DO;
255         LAMBDA = x[1];
256         DELTA  = x[2];
257         PRINT "ERROR - INITIAL VALUES ARE INVALID:" LABEL XI LAMBDA DELTA;
258         GOTO CONTINUE;
259      END;
260
261      LB=SBMEDIAN[i]-XI+0.01; /* LOWER BOUNDARY CONSTRAINT FOR LAMBDA */
262
263      UB=2*IV[i,1];            /* UPPER BOUNDARY CONSTRAINT FOR LAMBDA */
264                               /* SET AT 2 x INITIAL GUESS FOR LAMBDA  */
265                               /* USER CAN SET A DIFFERENT UPPER BOUND */
266
267      CON[1,1] = LB;           /* RESET VALUE IN CONSTRAINTS MATRIX */
268      CON[2,1] = UB;           /* RESET VALUE IN CONSTRAINTS MATRIX */
269
270      CALL NLPLM(RC,XR,"FCN",X,OPTN,CON,,,,"DERIV");     /* LEVENBERG-MARQUARDT */
271
272      L1_NORM = SUM(ABS(F));                             /* L1 NORM */
273      IF RC>0 THEN CONVERGE='YES'; ELSE CONVERGE='NO';   /* RC IS RETURN CODE */
274                                                         /* FROM NLPLM         */
275      PRINT LABEL XI LAMBDA GAMMA DELTA L1_NORM;
276      APPEND;                  /* ADD OBSERVATIONS TO OUTPUT DATASET */
277      CONTINUE:                /* GO TO NEXT OBSERVATION */
278
279   END;                        /* END OF DO LOOP PROCESSING */
280
281   QUIT;                       /* EXIT IML */
282
283   *-----    PRINT RESULTS;
284
285   PROC PRINT DATA=RESULTS;
286   RUN;
287
288   *-----    SAVE RESULTS TO AN EXCEL FILE;
289   *-----    USER SUPPLIED OUTFILE IN PROC EXPORT;
290
291   PROC EXPORT DATA= WORK.RESULTS
292              OUTFILE= "filename"
293              DBMS=EXCEL REPLACE;
294   RUN;
```

Appendix B

SAS Source Code for S_B Recovery 4parm

(Note: Line numbers are for reference and are not part of the program.)

```
 1  /*********************************************************************/
 2  /*                                                                 */
 3  /*                PROGRAM SB RECOVERY 4PARM (SAS version 9.1)       */
 4  /*                                                                 */
 5  /*   DESIGNED FOR TREE DIAMETER DISTRIBUTIONS, THIS PROGRAM USES A  */
 6  /*   PERCENTILE-MOMENT METHOD TO RECOVER ALL FOUR PARAMETERS OF     */
 7  /*   JOHNSON'S SB DISTRIBUTION: LOCATION PARAMETER (XI), RANGE      */
 8  /*   PARAMETER (LAMBDA) AND BOTH SHAPE PARAMETERS (GAMMA, DELTA).   */
 9  /*   INITIAL VALUES FOR XI, LAMBDA, AND DELTA MUST BE SUPPLIED TO   */
10  /*   START THE ITERATIVE LEVENBERG-MARQUARDT PROCEDURE.            */
11  /*                                                                 */
12  /*   INPUT VARIABLES:                                              */
13  /*                                                                 */
14  /*   ID = IDENTIFICATION CHARACTER VARIABLE FOR LABELING PURPOSES   */
15  /*   BA = STAND BASAL AREA PER UNIT AREA                           */
16  /*   NT = NUMBER OF TREES PER UNIT AREA                            */
17  /*   SBMEDIAN   = MEDIAN DIAMETER                                  */
18  /*   SBMEAN     = AVERAGE DIAMETER                                 */
19  /*   SBMUPRIME3 = THIRD NONCENTRAL MOMENT                          */
20  /*   IV_XI      = INITIAL OR STARTING VALUE FOR XI                 */
21  /*   IV_LAMBDA  = INITIAL OR STARTING VALUE FOR LAMBDA             */
22  /*   IV_DELTA   = INITIAL OR STARTING VALUE FOR DELTA              */
23  /*                                                                 */
24  /*   OUTPUT VARIABLES:                                             */
25  /*                                                                 */
26  /*   LABEL  = IDENTIFICATION CHARACTER VARIABLE                    */
27  /*   XI     = LOCATION PARAMETER                                   */
28  /*   LAMBDA = RANGE PARAMETER                                      */
29  /*   GAMMA  = SHAPE PARAMETER RELATED TO SKEWNESS                  */
30  /*   DELTA  = SHAPE PARAMETER                                      */
31  /*   L1_NORM = VALUE OF L1 NORM OF THE MINIMIZED FUNCTIONS         */
32  /*   CONVERGE = 'YES' OR 'NO' CHARACTER VARIABLE FOR CONVERGENCE   */
33  /*   RC = SAS RETURN CODE FROM IML ROUTINE NLPLM INDICATING WHICH  */
34  /*        CONVERGENCE CRITERIA WAS MET OR REASON FOR NONCONVERGENCE */
35  /*                                                                 */
36  /*   Reference:  Fonseca, T.F., Marques, C.P., and Parresol, B.R.  */
37  /*               2009. Describing maritime pine diameter           */
38  /*               distributions with Johnson's SB distribution      */
39  /*               using a new all-parameter recovery approach.      */
40  /*               Forest Science. 55(4): 367-373.                   */
41  /*                                                                 */
42  /*   Programmed by Bernard R. Parresol                            */
43  /*               USDA Forest Service                              */
44  /*               Southern Research Station                        */
45  /*               200 WT Weaver Boulevard                          */
46  /*               Asheville, NC 28804  USA                         */
47  /*                                                                 */
48  /*                         AND                                    */
49  /*                                                                 */
50  /*               Teresa Fidalgo Fonseca                           */
51  /*               Departamento de Ciências Florestais              */
52  /*                 e Arquitectura Paisagista                      */
53  /*               Universidade de Trás-os-Montes e Alto Douro      */
54  /*               Apartado 1013, 5001-801 Vila Real, Portugal      */
55  /*                                                                 */
56  /*********************************************************************/
57
58  OPTIONS NODATE SOURCE;
59
60  *-----    READ DATA FROM AN EXCEL FILE;
61  *-----    USER SUPPLIED DATAFILE IN PROC IMPORT;
```

```
62
63  PROC IMPORT OUT= WORK.ONE
64              DATAFILE= "filename"
65              DBMS=EXCEL REPLACE;
66       GETNAMES=YES;
67  RUN;
68
69  TITLE 'ALL PARAMETER RECOVERY SYSTEM FOR SB DISTRIBUTION';
70  * TITLE2 '-xxxxxxxxxx-';  /* <-- USER CAN ADD DESCRIPTIVE PROJECT TITLE */
71
72  PROC IML;  /* START MATRIX LANGUAGE */
73
74  START FCN(X)
75  GLOBAL(K,C,i,BA,NT,SBMEDIAN,SBMEAN,SBMUPRIME3,
76         XI,LAMBDA,DELTA,GAMMA,R,DM1,DM2,DM3,F);
77
78  /******************************************************/
79  /*                                                    */
80  /*      MODULE FCN IS CALLED BY PROCEDURE NLPLM TO    */
81  /*      EVALUATE THE LEFT-HAND SIDE OF EQUATIONS:     */
82  /*          FCN(XI,LAMBDA,DELTA) - SBMEAN = 0         */
83  /*          FCN(XI,LAMBDA,DELTA) - BA     = 0         */
84  /*          FCN(XI,LAMBDA,DELTA) - SBSIZE = 0         */
85  /*                                                    */
86  /******************************************************/
87
88  *------   SOLVE FOR GAMMA GIVEN ESTIMATES OF XI, LAMBDA, AND DELTA;
89
90       XI     = X[1];
91       LAMBDA = X[2];
92       DELTA  = X[3];
93       GAMMA  = DELTA*LOG(LAMBDA/(SBMEDIAN[i]-XI)-1);
94
95  *------   OBTAIN MOMENTS OF SB DISTRIBUTION;
96
97       A = {.M .P};                        /* LIMITS OF INTEGRATION    */
98       R = 1;                              /* EXPONENT FOR 1ST MOMENT  */
99       CALL QUAD(DM,"MOMENT",A)            /* NUMERICAL INTEGRATION    */
100        EPS=1E-10;
101      DM1 = C*DM;                         /* VALUE OF FIRST MOMENT    */
102
103      R = 2;                              /* EXPONENT FOR 2ND MOMENT  */
104      CALL QUAD(DM,"MOMENT",A)            /* NUMERICAL INTEGRATION    */
105        EPS=1E-10;
106      DM2 = C*DM;                         /* VALUE OF SECOND MOMENT   */
107
108      R = 3;                              /* EXPONENT FOR 3RD MOMENT  */
109      CALL QUAD(DM,"MOMENT",A)            /* NUMERICAL INTEGRATION    */
110        EPS=1E-10 PEAK=1 SCALE=0.1;
111      DM3 = C*DM;                         /* VALUE OF THIRD MOMENT    */
112
113  *------   COMPUTE VALUES OF FCN;
114
115       F = {0 0 0};
116      F[1] = XI + LAMBDA*DM1 - SBMEAN[i];
117      F[2] = (XI**2 + 2*XI*LAMBDA*DM1 + LAMBDA**2*DM2)*K^NT[i] - BA[i];
118      F[3] = XI**3 + 3*XI**2*LAMBDA*DM1 + 3*XI*LAMBDA**2*DM2 + LAMBDA**3*DM3
119             - SBMUPRIME3[i];
120      RETURN(F);
121  FINISH FCN;
```

```
122
123
124 START MOMENT(Z) GLOBAL(DELTA,GAMMA,R);
125
126 /***************************************************/
127 /*                                                 */
128 /*       MODULE MOMENT IS FOR EVALUATING THE       */
129 /*       MOMENTS OF THE SB DISTRIBUTION.           */
130 /*                                                 */
131 /***************************************************/
132
133   V = EXP(-.5*Z**2)/(1 + EXP((GAMMA-Z)/DELTA))**R;
134   RETURN(V);
135 FINISH MOMENT;
136
137
138 START PSEUDO(Z) GLOBAL(DELTA,GAMMA,R);
139
140 /***************************************************/
141 /*                                                 */
142 /*    MODULE PSEUDO IS FOR EVALUATING THE          */
143 /*    PSEUDO-MOMENTS OF THE SB DISTRIBUTION.       */
144 /*                                                 */
145 /***************************************************/
146
147   V = Z*EXP(-.5*Z**2)/(1 + EXP((GAMMA-Z)/DELTA))**R;
148   RETURN(V);
149 FINISH PSEUDO;
150
151
152 START DERIV(X) GLOBAL(K,C,i,XI,LAMBDA,GAMMA,DELTA,R,DM1,DM2,DM3,SBMEDIAN,NT);
153
154 /***************************************************/
155 /*                                                 */
156 /*   MODULE DERIV IS CALLED BY NLPLM               */
157 /*   TO EVALUATE THE PARTIAL DERIVATIVES OF        */
158 /*          FCN(XI,LAMBDA,DELTA) = SBMEAN          */
159 /*          FCN(XI,LAMBDA,DELTA) = BA              */
160 /*          FCN(XI,LAMBDA,DELTA) = SBSIZE          */
161 /*                                                 */
162 /***************************************************/
163
164 *-----   OBTAIN FOURTH MOMENT;
165
166      A = {.M .P};                       /* LIMITS OF INTEGRATION     */
167      R = 4;                             /* EXPONENT FOR 4TH MOMENT   */
168      CALL QUAD(DM,"MOMENT",A)           /* NUMERICAL INTEGRATION     */
169        EPS=1E-10 PEAK=1 SCALE=0.1;
170      DM4 = C*DM;                        /* VALUE OF FOURTH MOMENT    */
171
172 *-----   OBTAIN PSEUDO-MOMENTS;
173
174      R = 1;                             /* EXPONENT FOR 1ST PSEUDO-MOMENT */
175      CALL QUAD(PM,"PSEUDO",A)           /* NUMERICAL INTEGRATION          */
176        EPS=1E-10 PEAK=1 SCALE=0.1;
177      PM1 - C*PM;                        /* VALUE OF FIRST PSEUDO-MOMENT   */
178
```

```
179        R = 2;                              /* EXPONENT FOR 2ND PSEUDO-MOMENT */
180        CALL QUAD(PM,"PSEUDO",A)            /* NUMERICAL INTEGRATION         */
181          EPS=1E-10 PEAK=1 SCALE=0.1;
182        PM2 = C*PM;                         /* VALUE OF SECOND PSEUDO-MOMENT */
183
184        R = 3;                              /* EXPONENT FOR 3RD PSEUDO-MOMENT */
185        CALL QUAD(PM,"PSEUDO",A)            /* NUMERICAL INTEGRATION         */
186          EPS=1E-10 PEAK=1 SCALE=0.1;
187        PM3 = C*PM;                         /* VALUE OF THIRD PSEUDO-MOMENT  */
188
189        R = 4;                              /* EXPONENT FOR 4TH PSEUDO-MOMENT */
190        CALL QUAD(PM,"PSEUDO",A)            /* NUMERICAL INTEGRATION         */
191          EPS=1E-10 PEAK=1 SCALE=0.1;
192        PM4 = C*PM;                         /* VALUE OF FOURTH PSEUDO-MOMENT */
193
194 *-----   DEFINE COMMON ELEMENTS OF DERIVATIVES;
195
196        DM2_1 = DM2 - DM1;
197        DM3_2 = DM3 - DM2;
198        DM4_3 = DM4 - DM3;
199        DN1 = LAMBDA - SBMEDIAN[i] + XI;
200        DN2 = SBMEDIAN[i] - XI;
201
202 *-----   COMPUTE JACOBIAN MATRIX;
203
204          J = J(3,3,0);
205        J[1,1] = 1 + LAMBDA**2 * DM2_1 / (DN1 * DN2);          /* f1/XI     */
206        J[1,2] = DM1 + LAMBDA * DM2_1 / DN1;                   /* f1/LAMBDA */
207        J[1,3] = LAMBDA/DELTA**2*(PM2 - PM1);                  /* f1/DELTA  */
208        J[2,1] = (XI+LAMBDA*DM1+(XI*LAMBDA**2*DM2_1+LAMBDA**3
209                 *DM3_2) / (DN1 * DN2))*2*K*NT[i];              /* f2/XI     */
210        J[2,2] = (XI*DM1+LAMBDA*DM2+(XI*LAMBDA*DM2_1+LAMBDA**2
211                 *DM3_2) / DN1)*2*K*NT[i];                      /* f2/LAMBDA */
212        J[2,3] = LAMBDA/DELTA**2*(XI*(PM2 - PM1) + LAMBDA
213                 *(PM3 - PM2))*2*K*NT[i];                       /* f2/DELTA  */
214        J[3,1] = 3*(XI**2+2*XI*LAMBDA*DM1+LAMBDA**2*DM2+(XI**2
215                 *LAMBDA**2*DM2_1+2*XI*LAMBDA**3*DM3_2
216                 +LAMBDA**4*DM4_3) / (DN1 * DN2));              /* f3/XI     */
217        J[3,2] = 3*(XI**2*DM1+2*XI*LAMBDA*DM2+LAMBDA**2*DM3
218                 +(XI**2*LAMBDA*DM2_1+2*XI*LAMBDA**2*DM3_2
219                 +LAMBDA**3*DM4_3) / DN1);                      /* f3/LAMBDA */
220        J[3,3] = 3*LAMBDA/DELTA**2*(XI**2*(PM2 - PM1)
221                 +2*XI*LAMBDA*(PM3 - PM2)
222                 +LAMBDA**2*(PM4 - PM3));                       /* f3/DELTA  */
223        RETURN(J);
224 FINISH DERIV;
225
226
227 ***********   ----->  EXECUTE PROGRAM  <------   ***************;
228
229    LABEL = '12345';          /* TO LABEL OUTPUT, LENGTH CAN BE SET BY USER */
230 CONVERGE = '123';            /* INITIALIZE CHARACTER VARIABLE OF LENGTH 3  */
231
232 *-----   SET UP OUTPUT DATASET TO HOLD PARAMETER ESTIMATES AND RESULTS;
233
234 CREATE RESULTS VAR {LABEL XI LAMBDA GAMMA DELTA L1_NORM CONVERGE RC};
235
236 USE ONE;                     /* INPUT DATASET USED BY PROC IML */
237 READ ALL VAR{ID BA NT SBMEDIAN SBMEAN SBMUPRIME3 IV_XI IV_LAMBDA IV_DELTA};
238
```

```
239 NOBS = NROW(BA);                        /* NUMBER OF OBSERVATIONS */
240 IV = IV_XI||IV_LAMBDA||IV_DELTA;        /* MATRIX CONTAINING INITIAL VALUES */
241
242 *-----    INITIALIZATION;
243
244    PI = 4*ATAN(1);
245 *--K = PI/576;                  /* CONVERSION TO ft² - USE FOR ENGLISH SYSTEM    */
246     K = PI/40000;              /* CONVERSION TO m²  - USE FOR METRIC SYSTEM     */
247     C = 1/SQRT(2*PI);          /* CONSTANT FOR MOMENTS                          */
248
249    OPTN = {3 1};               /* OPTIONS VECTOR                                */
250                                /* 1ST VALUE IS NUMBER OF EQUATIONS IN SYSTEM    */
251                                /* 2ND VALUE DETERMINES AMOUNT OF PRINTED OUTPUT */
252                                /* 0=NO OUTPUT, 1=SUMMARIES & ITERATION HISTORY  */
253
254    TC = {400 1000};            /* TERMINATION CRITERIA VECTOR       */
255                                /* 1ST VALUE IS MAX ITERATIONS       */
256                                /* 2ND VALUE IS MAX FUNCTION CALLS   */
257
258
259 /*---   BOUNDARY CONDITIONS AND LINEAR RESTRICTIONS ARE IMPOSED WITH    ---*/
260 /*---   THE BLC MATRIX OR BOUNDARY & LINEAR CONSTRAINTS MATRIX.         ---*/
261 /*---   CONSTRAINTS MUST USE >= AND <= INEQUALITIES, NOT > OR <         ---*/
262 /*---   INEQUALITIES. WITH THIS IN MIND, WE USE THE FOLLOWING FACTS TO  ---*/
263 /*---   CONSTRUCT THE NECESSARY BLC MATRIX. GAMMA (G) IS A FUNCTION OF  ---*/
264 /*---   THE OTHER 3 PARAMETERS XI, LAMBDA(L) AND DELTA (D) PLUS THE     ---*/
265 /*---   MEDIAN DIAMETER (SBMEDIAN), i.e. G = D×LN(L/(SBMEDIAN-XI)-1).   ---*/
266 /*---   DIAMETER CAN NOT BE LESS THAN ZERO. FROM THE EQUATION IT IS     ---*/
267 /*---   OBVIOUS THAT XI MUST BE LESS THAN SBMEDIAN TO AVOID AN ILLEGAL  ---*/
268 /*---   LOG ARGUMENT, HENCE 0<=XI<SBMEDIAN. ALTERNATIVELY, ONE CAN USE  ---*/
269 /*---   OBSERVED MINIMUM DIAMETER AS AN UPPER BOUND CONSTRAINT FOR XI.  ---*/
270 /*---   THE EQUATION ALSO REVEALS THAT L/(SBMEDIAN-XI) > 1 TO AVOID AN  ---*/
271 /*---   ILLEGAL LOG ARGUMENT, THUS SBMEDIAN-XI < L. BECAUSE XI AND L    ---*/
272 /*---   ARE SIMULTANEOUSLY ESTIMATED, THIS GIVES THE LINEAR RESTRICTION ---*/
273 /*---   XI + L > SBMEDIAN. AS A PRACTICAL MATTER THE RANGE SHOULD BE     ---*/
274 /*---   RESTRICTED. A REASONABLE UPPER BOUND IS 2×INITIAL GUESS FOR L.  ---*/
275 /*---   BY DEFINITION, D > 0. GATHERING ALL THIS TOGETHER, WE HAVE:     ---*/
276 /*---                                                                   ---*/
277 /*---                   0 <= XI <  SBMEDIAN                             ---*/
278 /*---                        L  <= 2 x IV_L   (IV IS INITIAL VALUE)    ---*/
279 /*---                   0 <  D                                         ---*/
280 /*---                   XI + L  >  SBMEDIAN                            ---*/
281 /*---                                                                   ---*/
282 /*---   BECAUSE CONSTRAINTS MUST BE EXPRESSED AS <= OR >=, WE NEED TO   ---*/
283 /*---   MAKE SMALL ADJUSTMENTS. OUR FINAL CONSTRAINTS ARE:             ---*/
284 /*---                                                                   ---*/
285 /*---                   0 <= XI <= SBMEDIAN - 0.01                     ---*/
286 /*---                        L  <= 2 x IV_L                            ---*/
287 /*---              0.01 <= D                                           ---*/
288 /*---                   XI + L  >= SBMEDIAN + 0.01                     ---*/
289
290
291    BLC = {0  . 1E-2  . . ,        /* BLC MATRIX, ELEMENTS OF ROW 1 ARE LOWER */
292                                   /* BOUNDS FOR XI, LAMBDA & DELTA. ELEMENTS */
293          1  1   .  1  . };       /* OF ROW 2 ARE UPPER BOUNDS FOR XI,       */
294                                   /* LAMBDA, DELTA. ELEMENTS OF ROW 3 ARE    */
295                                   /* USED FOR THE LINEAR RESTRICTION. A '.'  */
296                                   /* OR MISSING VALUE MEANS NO BOUNDARY OR   */
297                                   /* IS A PLACE HOLDER.                      */
```

```
298
299  *-----     PROCESS OBSERVATIONS;
300
301  DO i = 1 TO NOBS;              /* LOOP THROUGH OBSERVATIONS */
302
303     LABEL = ID[i];
304     X=IV[i,];                   /* INITAL VALUES VECTOR FOR PARAMETERS */
305
306  *-----     CHECK VALIDITY OF INITIAL VALUES;
307
308     IF X[1] < 0 | X[1] > SBMEDIAN[i]-0.01 | X[2] < SBMEDIAN[i]-X[1]+0.01
309       | X[3] < 0.01 THEN DO;
310       XI     = X[1];
311       LAMBDA = X[2];
312       DELTA  = X[3];
313       PRINT "ERROR - INITIAL VALUES ARE INVALID:" LABEL XI LAMBDA DELTA;
314       GOTO CONTINUE;
315     END;
316
317     UB_XI = SBMEDIAN[i]-0.01;  /* UPPER BOUNDARY CONSTRAINT FOR XI */
318
319     UB_LAMBDA = 2*IV[i,2];     /* UPPER BOUNDARY CONSTRAINT FOR LAMBDA */
320                                /* SET AT 2 x INITIAL GUESS FOR LAMBDA */
321                                /* USER CAN SET A DIFFERENT UPPER BOUND */
322
323     LR = SBMEDIAN[i]+0.01;     /* LINEAR RESTRICTION */
324
325     BLC[2,1] = UB_XI;          /* RESET VALUE IN CONSTRAINTS MATRIX */
326     BLC[2,2] = UB_LAMBDA;      /* RESET VALUE IN CONSTRAINTS MATRIX */
327     BLC[3,5] = LR;             /* RESET VALUE IN CONSTRAINTS MATRIX */
328
329     CALL NLPLM(RC,XR,"FCN",X,OPTN,BLC,TC,,,"DERIV");   /* LEVENBERG-MARQUARDT */
330
331     IF XI < 1E-7 THEN XI=0;    /* ROUND SMALL VALUES OF XI TO ZERO */
332     L1_NORM = SUM(ABS(F));                             /* L1 NORM */
333     IF RC>0 THEN CONVERGE='YES'; ELSE CONVERGE='NO';   /* RC IS RETURN CODE */
334                                                        /* FROM NLPLM */
335     PRINT LABEL XI LAMBDA GAMMA DELTA L1_NORM;
336     APPEND;                    /* ADD OBSERVATIONS TO OUTPUT DATASET */
337     CONTINUE:                  /* GO TO NEXT OBSERVATION */
338
339  END;                          /* END OF DO LOOP PROCESSING */
340
341  QUIT;                         /* EXIT IML */
342
343  *-----     PRINT RESULTS;
344
345  PROC PRINT DATA=RESULTS;
346  RUN;
347
348  *-----     SAVE RESULTS TO AN EXCEL FILE;
349  *-----     USER SUPPLIED OUTFILE IN PROC EXPORT;
350
351  PROC EXPORT DATA= WORK.RESULTS
352             OUTFILE= "filename"
353             DBMS=EXCEL REPLACE;
354  RUN;
```